# CONTROVERSIES

CREATIVE C EDUCATION

THE
WAR ON
TERROR

BY TERESA WIMMER

Published by Creative Education
P.O. Box 227, Mankato, Minnesota 56002
Creative Education is an imprint of The Creative Company
www.thecreativecompany.us

Art direction by Rita Marshall
Design and production by The Design Lab
Printed by Corporate Graphics in the United States of America

Photographs by Alamy (Peter Jordan, Visions of America, LLC),
Corbis (Sygma), DefenseImagery (Master Sgt. Shane A. Cuomo),
Dreamstime (Aidar Ayazbayev), Getty Images (AFP, Ahmad
Al-Rubaye/AFP, Scott Barbour, Reg Burkett/Express, Veronique
de Viguerie/Edit, David Furst/AFP, Ramzi Haidar/AFP, Stephen
Hilger/Bloomberg, Hulton Archive, Yoray Liberman, Rich
Lipski/*The Washington Post*, Win Mcnamee/AFP, John Moore,
Syamsul Bahri Muhammad, Oleg Nikishin, Pool Photo/Newsmakers,
Paul J. Richards/AFP, Mark Wilson, Roger L. Wollenberg-Pool),
iStockphotos (Andrew Robinson, Dane Wirtzfeld), U.S. Air
Force (Lt. Col Leslie Pratt)

Library of Congress Cataloging-in-Publication Data
Wimmer, Teresa.
Controversies / by Teresa Wimmer.
p. cm. — (The war on terror)
Includes bibliographical references and index.
ISBN 978-1-60818-098-1
1. Terrorism—Prevention—Government policy—United States—
Juvenile literature. 2. War on Terrorism, 2001-2009—Moral
and ethical aspects—Juvenile literature. 3. Iraq War, 2003—
Juvenile literature. I. Title.

HV6432.W557 2011
363.325'170973—dc22     2010033629

CPSIA: 110310 P01387

First Edition
9 8 7 6 5 4 3 2 1

# TABLE OF CONTENTS

The events of September 11, 2001, led to a conflict that soon had American troops engaged in combat on the streets of cities in Afghanistan and Iraq.

I n the late 1980s, a conflict rooted in terrorism began to rear its head on a global scale. This strife pitted Islamic fundamentalists, radical religious **militants** springing primarily from nations in the Middle East, against the countries and culture of the Western world. Spilling across parts of four decades, this conflict—which came to be known from the Western perspective as "The War on Terror"—grew from bombings and guerrilla combat into the first large-scale war of the 21st century, marked by the infamous events of September 11, 2001, and intensive military campaigns in the countries of Afghanistan and Iraq.

The War on Terror, unlike most previous wars, did not involve traditional warfare between uniformed soldiers of different countries, with clearly defined motives and goals. Rather, the war unfolded as a complicated struggle involving hidden enemies and sharply contrasting cultures and beliefs. When the war began in earnest in 2001, the actions taken by Islamic terror groups, such as waging war in the name of Islam and killing fellow Muslims, caused great angst among people of the Middle East. Meanwhile, in Western nations, tighter security measures, the expansion of governmental powers, new methods of warfare, and the treatment of prisoners generated intense controversy. Over the years, numerous decisions and actions were hotly debated, emphasizing the gulf between the ideas and viewpoints held by both sides.

# CHAPTER ONE

# QUESTIONABLE MOTIVES

The War on Terror has generated as much controversy as any war in history. Even the use of the term "war" has been controversial, since some people believe there is no single group whose defeat can truly lead to victory, and it is unlikely that international terrorism can be ended using military means. Other people say that "terrorism" is not an enemy but a tactic and that the phrase "War on Terror" undermines important differences between the combatants facing the U.S. military and its Western allies—for example, homegrown **insurgents** and international **jihadists**. Some

note that terrorism exists in so many forms that a War on Terror can have no true end. In a speech given on September 20, 2001, U.S. president George W. Bush laid out the objectives of the War on Terror by saying it "will not end until every terrorist group of global reach has been found, stopped, and defeated." In that same speech, he called the war "a task that does not end."

Long before the start of the War on Terror, America's foreign policies had generated controversy, especially as they pertained to intervention in the affairs of Middle Eastern countries. During World War II (1939–1945),

Nearly all Americans united behind president George W. Bush immediately after "9/11," but his leadership would later divide the country.

Mohammad Reza Shah Pahlavi, as the king of Iran, ran an oppressive monarchy in which Iranian citizens did not have freedom of speech, and many poor and working-class people did not benefit from the country's vast oil profits. In the late 1940s, reformer Mohammad Mosaddeq, a popular public figure, led a movement to national-ize (put under govern-ment control) Iran's oil industry and was elected prime minister in 1951. Because America had an interest in getting oil from Iran, and because it was in the midst of the **Cold War** and did not want to risk Iran's forming an alliance with the Soviet Union, the U.S. overthrew Mosaddeq and restored Pahlavi (who had long been on good terms with the West) to power. This action compelled many Iranians to believe that America's main inter-est in countries such as Iran was oil, not the well-being of its people. Many people around the world began to see the U.S. as attempting to play the role of "interna-tional police," stepping in to mediate conflicts within foreign countries, such as Iran, with-out consulting the people of that nation.

Mohammad Reza Shah Pahlavi

A stern figure known for his hard-line policies, the ayatollah Ruhollah Khomeini became the face of Islam to many Westerners in the 1980s.

## IRANIAN REVOLUTION

In 1979, Mohammad Reza Shah Pahlavi, the pro-Western ruler of Iran, was overthrown in a revolution and replaced by radical Islamic cleric Ruhollah Khomeini. Khomeini quickly declared Iran an Islamic Republic and banned such "corrupt" elements as gambling, alcohol, and nightclubs. In 1989, Khomeini issued a religious decree calling for the assassination of British author Salman Rushdie on the grounds that his book *The Satanic Verses*, which advocated that prayers be made to pre-Islamic goddesses, was **blasphemous**. This suggested to Western nations that Iran aimed to impose its will internationally.

The Kaaba, a square building in Mecca, Saudi Arabia, is the holiest site in Islam; when Muslims pray, they always face toward it.

## SAUDI CONNECTIONS

Although Saudi Arabia and the U.S. are allies, the "9/11" attacks complicated their relationship. Of the 19 al Qaeda hijackers, 15 were Saudi citizens. Also, Osama bin Laden, who led al Qaeda until his death in May 2011, was born in Saudi Arabia. Crown Prince Abdullah, Saudi Arabia's acting ruler, immediately condemned the 9/11 attacks. However, some wealthy Saudi businessmen continued to funnel financial aid to al Qaeda after 9/11. Money contributed by wealthy Saudi citizens also helped to fuel the resurgence of the Taliban in 2003.

For decades, one of America's key allies in the Middle East has been the kingdom of Saudi Arabia. Many people see this alliance as contradictory, since Saudi Arabia has an **absolute monarchy**, holds some of the strictest laws (based upon Islam) in the world, and has been the birthplace of many terrorists. Saudi Arabia is also the world's leading oil producer, which helps to explain its appeal as an ally to the West. Osama bin Laden, who later founded the terrorist group al Qaeda, grew up in Saudi Arabia and funded many young Arabs who fought in conflicts such as the 1979 Soviet invasion of Afghanistan and subsequent decade-long war. During the war, in order to oppose Soviet expansion in the area, the U.S. provided financial aid and weapons to the **mujahideen** and supported fighters such as bin Laden, some of whom later became anti-U.S. terrorists. Some critics said that by doing this, the U.S. demonstrated that it was willing to endorse violent or undemocratic groups as long as it served America's interests.

Osama bin Laden

After the Soviets were finally driven out of Afghanistan in 1989, the U.S. and other Western nations stopped sending financial aid to Afghanistan, and the country soon found itself in the midst of a civil war between various factions of the mujahideen. This chaos made Afghans eager for stability and made the country vulnerable to new rule. It was because of this vulnerability that the Taliban—a radical, fundamentalist Islamic group—was able to rise to power in Afghanistan in 1994, and it imposed its harsh rules over the Afghan people.

Under the Taliban (Arabic for "Islamic students who seek knowledge"), women were required to wear **burkas** in public, and men were required to grow beards. Thieves were punished by having their hands cut off, singing and music were forbidden, and Afghans who did not pray five times a day could be sent to prison. Women were denied an education and could be stoned to death for having affairs. The Taliban justified its laws by arguing that a return to strict Islamic practices was the only way to institute order and bring the country back from the brink of disaster. "The group promoted itself," said American political scientist Seth G. Jones, "as a new force for honesty and unity, and many Afghans … saw the Taliban as the desperately needed balm of peace and stability." Many Westerners and Muslims alike, however, came to reject the Taliban's violations of human rights.

Terrorist groups such as al Qaeda also were viewed unfavorably by many Muslims

Mujahideen fighters stand on a downed helicopter in Afghanistan in 1987; militants used U.S.-provided, shoulder-fired missiles to fight the Soviets.

## IMPORTANT VICTORY

In 1979, the Soviet Union invaded Afghanistan, attempting to secure a pro-Soviet government in that country. From the perspective of many people in the Middle East, the invasion represented just the latest example of non-Muslim countries trying to control Islamic nations. In response, the mujahideen fought hard to drive the Soviets out of their country, finally succeeding in 1989. For many Muslim fighters (including Osama bin Laden) who would later become terrorists, the victory over the Soviets gave them the confidence that Muslims would eventually be able to drive Western nations completely out of the Middle East.

in the 1990s. Al Qaeda made its name known with such attacks as the 1998 bombings of U.S. embassies in Kenya and Tanzania and truly earned global renown with the September 11, 2001, attacks on New York's World Trade Center and the **Pentagon** in Washington, D.C. In the sixth century, the prophet Muhammad instructed all Muslims to create a just society in which people were not exploited and did not suffer. Islamic beliefs, say most Muslims, are meant to unite the worldwide community of Muslims, and it is the duty of all Muslims to spread the message of Islam peacefully. According to the Qur'an (or Koran), Islam's holy book, any Islamic government created through violence is not legitimate. Although many people in the Middle East agree with key points made by al Qaeda and other radical Islamic groups—especially regarding Western involvement in the Middle East and support of oppressive governments—they do not harbor any ill will against Western citizens and do not condone the violence of terrorism. To them, it is a desecration of Islam itself.

The 9/11 attack on the Pentagon received less media coverage than that on the World Trade Center, in part because no video captured the impact.

## THE D.C. SNIPER

The 9/11 attacks made some Americans fear ordinary Muslims. John Allen Muhammad reinforced such fears. In the fall of 2002, Muhammad—who was born John Allen Williams but changed his surname after becoming a Muslim—was arrested for killing 10 people along the Capital Beltway highway in the Washington, D.C., area by firing a rifle from his car. Authorities claimed that Muhammad, a U.S. veteran of the Persian Gulf War, admitted to modeling himself after Osama bin Laden. Muhammad was found guilty of the murders and executed in November 2009.

# CHAPTER TWO

# HOME CONTROVERSIES

Immediately after the 9/11 attacks, U.S. president George W. Bush vowed to bring those responsible to justice, but many of the ways in which his administration pursued justice would prove controversial. The U.S. Congress passed the Uniting and Strengthening America by Providing Appropriate Tools Required to Intercept and Obstruct Terrorism (USA Patriot) Act in the fall of 2001, which gave the federal government sweeping powers—more power than it had ever had before—to act quickly without consulting Congress or the Supreme Court. Under the provisions of the Patriot Act, the Bush administration conducted secret searches of U.S. citizens, monitored Islamic religious and political groups in America, and questioned hundreds of Muslim students in the U.S. Such controversial actions led some Middle Eastern critics to allege that the War on Terror was actually a "War on Islam."

The Bush administration, however, defended its actions. It argued that the traditional tools of law enforcement, such as search warrants, criminal indictments, and federal trials, did not go far enough—or lend themselves to fast enough action—when dealing with a stateless enemy such as al Qaeda, whose suicide hijackers had easily blended in with the U.S. civilian population before 9/11. Supporters of the Patriot Act asserted that aggressive attacks such

Despite the controversies it generated, the Patriot Act was maintained in 2006 when President Bush signed a reauthorization bill into law.

PROTECTING THE HOMELAND

## WATERBOARDING

One of the most controversial interrogation methods used on detainees at Guantánamo Bay was waterboarding, a process in which suspects are held in water or have water poured on their face to make them believe they will drown. Khalid Sheikh Mohammed, the al Qaeda mastermind of the 9/11 attacks, was reportedly waterboarded 183 times before the practice was banned in January 2009. U.S. president Barack Obama announced that Mohammed and four other 9/11 terrorists should stand trial in civilian court, although officials, as of late 2010, were still trying to decide on a location.

The Guantánamo Bay detention center, which has held such infamous figures as Khalid Sheikh Mohammed, was often criticized for its secrecy.

as 9/11 justified an equally aggressive response, and that the U.S. Constitution gave the president broad discretionary power when national security was threatened.

When the U.S. led a multinational invasion of Afghanistan in October 2001, the **coalition** forces were able to kill or capture many members of al Qaeda and the Taliban. A decision then had to be made on where to hold these prisoners. The Bush administration decided on a detention center at Guantánamo Bay, a U.S. naval station in Cuba, because the U.S. federal courts had no jurisdiction over law-suits filed by people captured, tried, and convicted outside the U.S. This meant that if the detainees questioned why they were being held, they could not file a lawsuit against the U.S. government. Some people, including numerous U.S. lawyers, said this practice under-mined the basic legal rights to which all U.S. prisoners were entitled.

Bush broadened the power of the presidency even further when he signed an order on November 13, 2001, authorizing the use of **military tribunals** to try non-Americans in the U.S. The tribunals were applicable to all non-citizens whom the Bush administration had reason to believe were affiliated with al Qaeda or had assisted with acts of terrorism inside the U.S. In these trials, the president would choose who to try, evidence based on hearsay would be admissible, a majority of votes would be enough for a guilty verdict, and no appeals would be allowed in U.S. courts. Bush kept the military tribunals a secret until the last minute—not even **secretary of state** Colin Powell or national security advisor Condoleezza Rice knew about the

plans until after Bush had signed the order.

Almost immediately, these new, broad executive powers generated hot debate. In order for the U.S. government to deprive an individual of his liberties (which many people agreed was sometimes necessary during wartime), Congress needed to pass a bill, the president had to sign it, and the Supreme Court had to deem the act constitutional. As such, prominent lawyers in the U.S. argued that the military tribunals were unconstitutional and illegal because the president did not consult Congress first.

Critics also condemned the Bush administration for claiming, without any public debate, the authority to indefinitely detain (and withhold the identities of) U.S. citizens who were suspected of having terrorist connections.

Critics also charged that the Bush administration invented new terminology to create loopholes to get around established international laws. The administration used the term "enemy combatants" to define Taliban and al Qaeda members and those who aided them, because the Taliban was never internationally recognized as a government, and al Qaeda was stateless. Previously, international law had defined prisoners as either "lawful combatants" (members of a nation's armed forces authorized to engage in combat) or "unlawful combatants" (people who are not authorized to participate in combat but commit aggressive acts against a foreign enemy). However, critics charged that by using the term "enemy combatant," the Bush administration assumed the right to apply that term to anyone—even U.S. citizens suspected of having terrorist ties—and to not be confined to the limitations of the **Geneva Conventions**. "The

## THE TALIBAN AMERICAN

John Walker Lindh grew up in a Christian household in California. At 16, he converted to Islam and shortly thereafter left for Yemen to study the Qur'an. In 2000, he asked to join the Taliban but was told to attend al Qaeda training camps first. When the U.S. bombardment of Afghanistan began after 9/11, Lindh was taken prisoner along with 3,000 other Taliban soldiers, becoming known as the "Taliban American." He apologized for fighting alongside the Taliban but in 2002 was sentenced to 20 years in prison.

[Bush] administration seemed to view the law as an obstacle to getting the job done," said one such critic, Georgetown University law professor David Cole. However, attorney general Alberto Gonzales defended the administration's actions, saying that enemy combatant "detention is not an act of punishment ... but serves the important purpose of preventing enemy combatants from continuing their attacks."

Although most of the world sympathized with the U.S. after the 9/11 attacks and agreed that the attackers must be brought to justice, this support began to wane as many people questioned the Bush administration's treatment of detainees. The first planeload of suspected terrorists landed at Guantánamo Bay on January 11, 2002, and by early 2003, more than 600 were being held there, most indefinitely and without having been charged with a specific crime. This led some activist groups to come to the detainees' aid. In February 2002, the Center for Constitutional Rights filed a lawsuit against the U.S. government on behalf of the Guantánamo Bay prisoners. In June 2004, the U.S. Supreme Court ruled that all individuals held at Guantánamo Bay had the right to know—and challenge in U.S. courts—the reason for their detention.

Public pressure also led to improved military tribunal procedures in 2003. Under the new rules, defendants were presumed innocent until proven guilty, detainees had the right to hire civilian lawyers to defend them (instead of using military-appointed lawyers), a unanimous verdict was needed

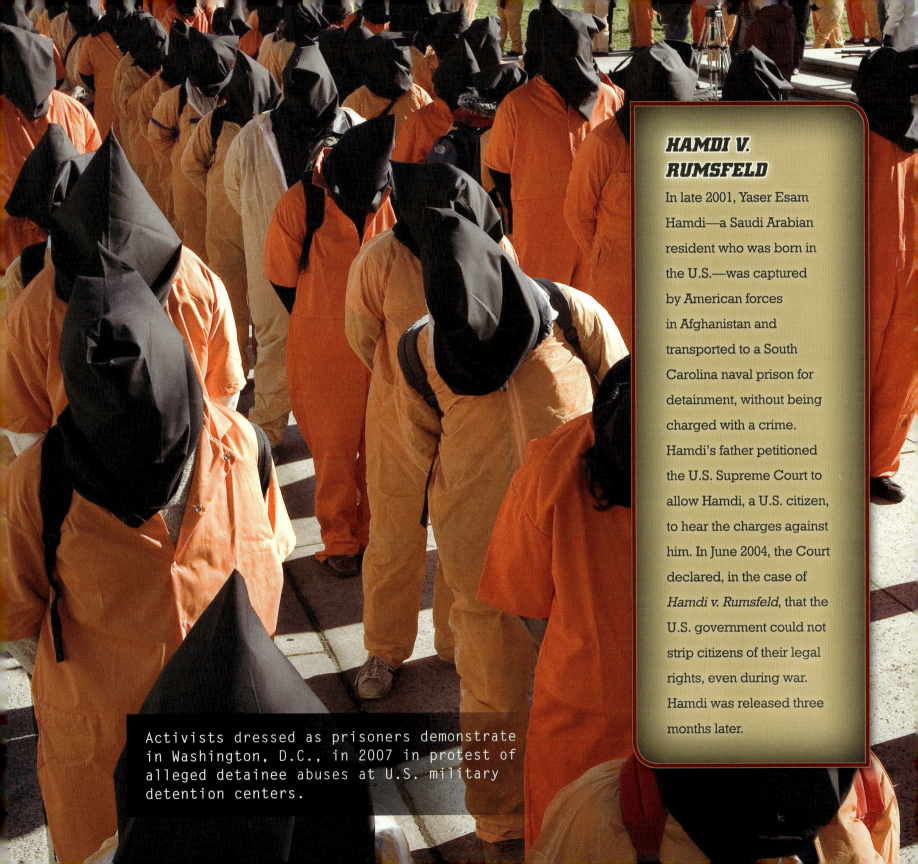

## HAMDI V. RUMSFELD

In late 2001, Yaser Esam Hamdi—a Saudi Arabian resident who was born in the U.S.—was captured by American forces in Afghanistan and transported to a South Carolina naval prison for detainment, without being charged with a crime. Hamdi's father petitioned the U.S. Supreme Court to allow Hamdi, a U.S. citizen, to hear the charges against him. In June 2004, the Court declared, in the case of *Hamdi v. Rumsfeld*, that the U.S. government could not strip citizens of their legal rights, even during war. Hamdi was released three months later.

Activists dressed as prisoners demonstrate in Washington, D.C., in 2007 in protest of alleged detainee abuses at U.S. military detention centers.

in order to administer the death penalty, and a limited appeals process was put into place. The previously secretive trials were also partly opened to media coverage.

The governmental policies of some U.S. allies also came under scrutiny as the War on Terror progressed. In Great Britain, critics claimed that prime minister Tony Blair used the war as a justification for limiting civil liberties, especially the right of **habeas corpus**, which was first set forth in the Magna Carta, the foundational document of English law. Critics charged that Blair placed limitations on free speech by passing laws forbidding protests near Parliament, detained prisoners in Belmarsh Prison (in southeast London) without trial, and reduced checks on police power—in effect, broadening governmental authority in many of the same ways that the Bush administration had. As the War on Terror intensified and moved to new fronts, these controversies proved to be just the beginning.

British prime minister Tony Blair

More than 10,000 Humvees were used by coalition forces during the 2003 invasion of Iraq and subsequent Iraq War.

## THE HUMMER

A new kind of military vehicle was introduced during the 1991 Persian Gulf War—the Humvee. This large, powerful, all-terrain vehicle was used to transport troops and supplies over the rough landscape of the Middle East. Some Americans found these rugged vehicles appealing, so General Motors (GM) soon produced a civilian model called the Hummer. The Hummer, which averaged only nine miles (14 km) per gallon, later came under fire from environmental groups, and sales began to fall. GM discontinued the Hummer in 2009.

# CHAPTER THREE

# ON TO IRAQ

In early 2002, after the U.S.-led coalition forced the Taliban from power and had key al Qaeda and Taliban leaders trapped in the Afghan mountains, the Bush administration debated where to take the War on Terror next. It decided on Iraq. President Saddam Hussein's oppressive **regime** in Iraq had a long history of human rights violations. It had also repeatedly refused to allow weapons inspectors into the country to see if Hussein had complied with **United Nations (UN)** demands to destroy all **weapons of mass destruction (WMD)**—a stipulation imposed by the UN after Iraq was defeated in the 1991 Persian Gulf War. Because of this, Bush and Blair considered Hussein an imminent threat to both Middle Eastern and global security, and they felt it was their duty to forcibly remove him from power. With the

Iraqi president Saddam Hussein

Many people who opposed Western involvement in the Persian Gulf War and the U.S-led invasion of Iraq in 2003 accused the West of coveting oil.

## NO BLOOD FOR OIL

When Iraq, under president Saddam Hussein, invaded Kuwait in August 1990, U.S. troops were deployed to the Middle East to protect Saudi Arabia and free Kuwait, which both held large oil reserves. Fewer than half of polled Americans favored going to war before January 15, 1991, but after the Persian Gulf War began, 75 percent believed that the U.S. had done the right thing. However, people around the world had different reactions. In western Europe, young people carried signs demanding "No Blood for Oil," suggesting that the U.S. went to war mainly to protect Saudi oil fields.

## PREDATOR DRONES

After 2006, America's increasing use of unmanned aerial vehicles (UAVs) to seek out and kill al Qaeda and Taliban militants generated controversy. Commonly called Predator drones, for one of the most popular models, UAVs are aircraft that are programmed to survey an area, with the capability of dropping bombs or firing missiles on targets. U.S. officials estimated that drones killed more than 500 militants from 2008 to 2010. However, because UAVs do not use human pilots, some critics charge that their use is inhumane or even cowardly, since operators can kill from thousands of miles away, without risking their own lives.

Predator drones proved highly effective in the war in Afghanistan, as they could find and strike terrorists and insurgents in hard-to-navigate terrain.

support of Congress, the Bush administration stated that it intended to remove "a regime that developed and used weapons of mass destruction, that harbored and supported terrorists, committed outrageous human rights abuses, and defied the just demands of the United Nations and the world."

On March 20, 2003, U.S. and British forces—along with troops from Australia and Poland—launched Operation Iraqi Freedom with air strikes on the capital city of Baghdad. The invasion guaranteed immediate and global controversy, however, since the **UN Security Council**, which had authorized the invasion of Afghanistan after 9/11, did not support an invasion of Iraq. Internationally, and even among sizable segments of the U.S. and British populations, the war in Iraq did not find much support. Some charged that the U.S. and Britain had violated international law and undermined the authority of the UN by invading a nation that had not launched an attack on either country. Critics said the coalition was guilty of committing a war of aggression and that the U.S. was setting a dangerous precedent under which any nation could justify the invasion of another. U.S.

A convoy of UN weapons inspectors conduct a search of sites near Baghdad, Iraq, in 2003 for concealed missiles or WMD.

counterterrorism expert Bruce Riedel suggested that Bush had lost sight of the true enemy, noting, "The president chose to declare war not on al Qaeda but on 'terrorism,' a concept that he and vice president Dick Cheney arrived at by confusing 9/11 with Saddam Hussein's Iraq."

A month after Baghdad fell in May 2003, the U.S.-led Iraq Survey Group (ISG) was established to search for WMD developed and concealed under Hussein's regime. In September 2004, the ISG issued a report stating that Iraq had indeed destroyed its WMD after the Persian Gulf War and had not developed any new chemical or biological weapons. As international media ran news stories about the ISG findings, many critics of the Iraq invasion charged that the

political leadership in the U.S. and Britain had purposefully misled the public about Iraq's WMD in order to justify the invasion. The lack of WMD further served to lend evidence to claims by Islamic fundamentalists that the Western world was intent on waging a war on Islam and would use any means—or excuses—necessary to overthrow Muslim countries.

It was at about this time that stories of prisoner mistreatment began to come out of the Abu Ghraib prison in Iraq, raising new ethics questions. In April 2004, the television program *60 Minutes* first aired photographs showing the apparent abuse of Iraqi prisoners inside Abu Ghraib at the hands of American military personnel. The photos depicted U.S. guards forcing some prisoners to wear a leash, some to strip off their clothes and endure humiliat-ing poses, and others to be threatened with snarling guard dogs. The photos shocked and outraged people around the world, embarrassing Americans in particular. Some techniques allegedly used by the U.S. military at Abu Ghraib and Guantánamo Bay—such as forcing pris-oners to curse Islam and Allah during their interrogations—seemed especially designed, to many in the Middle East, to exploit the sen-sitivities of the Muslim culture. Deeply ashamed, some prisoners chose to commit suicide.

This reported torture of prisoners raised further discussion about human rights. The Bush administration and its supporters said that this new struggle against terrorism required new techniques. To that end, they argued that harsh interrogation techniques were sometimes necessary to obtain potentially life-saving information from prisoners of high importance. However, many people worldwide argued that the U.S. and its allies, despite the murky details of the war, should be above using torture—that violating the same kind of basic human rights the U.S. claimed to stand for made America no more righteous

The Abu Ghraib prison was infamous even before the Iraq War, as many Iraqis had been tortured and killed there under Saddam Hussein's rule.

## PUBLIC APOLOGY

When news of the Abu Ghraib prison scandal broke, U.S. president George W. Bush issued an apology to the American public and the rest of the world, promising that the offenders would be punished. After an investigation, 13 American military service members were discharged, 54 suffered lesser punishments, and 57 were **court-martialed**. Some people, however, did not think the government went far enough in its disciplinary action against the guilty guards and interrogators, and the scandal incited further worldwide criticism of the U.S. presence in Iraq.

The 2007 assassination of Benazir Bhutto was a blow to many in the Middle East, as she had been the first woman to be elected leader of any Muslim nation.

than the terrorists. In response to the prison scandal, Congress passed the Detainee Treatment Act of 2005, which prohibited the "cruel, inhumane, or degrading treatment or punishment" of detainees.

As allegations of prisoner abuse became public, and as claims were made that the U.S. and its allies had purposefully misled the public about the existence of Iraq's WMD, the people of Iraq—who saw their country fall into chaos—gained much sympathy from the rest of the world, especially from within the Middle East. The combination of these events put international support for the war at an all-time low. According to a report commissioned by the U.S.-sponsored Coalition Provisional Authority in Iraq, before the release of the abuse photos, 63 percent of Iraqis supported the U.S. presence there; afterward, that number plummeted to 9 percent. In addition, no firm link was ever found to have existed between al Qaeda and Saddam Hussein's regime in Iraq, and perceptions of U.S. **unilateralism** and arrogance strained relationships between America and some of its longtime Western allies, including France and Germany.

## THE PEOPLE'S CANDIDATE

By 2007, many people in Pakistan were tired of the strict military rule of General Pervez Musharraf, who had served as Pakistan's president for six years, and wanted greater freedom and democracy. Many saw former Pakistani prime minister Benazir Bhutto as their greatest hope for change. Under the Pakistan Peoples Party, Bhutto hoped for reelection in 2008. When she was assassinated in December 2007, many Pakistanis were devastated and blamed Musharraf and the Pakistani army. Rising criticism eventually led Musharraf to resign as president in August 2008.

# CHAPTER FOUR

# SEARCHING FOR AN END

From the summer of 2003 through the fall of 2007, some nine months after President Bush authorized a troop surge in Iraq to help support the country's newly elected democratic government, insurgent attacks against coalition forces grew more frequent and violent. In Afghanistan, too, the fighting intensified. Despite their impressive intelligence capabilities, coalition forces did not always obtain accurate information in identifying terrorists and insurgents, and Iraqi and Afghan civilians sometimes became caught in the crossfire. The UN estimated that 34,000 civilians in Iraq were killed in 2006, and 5 percent of the country's population became homeless refugees. In Afghanistan, thousands of civilians became casualties of the rampant bombings and gunfire. Critics of the war decried these statistics, but supporters said that, as in any war, **collateral damage** was sometimes inevitable, despite improvements in technology and the best efforts to prevent civilian deaths.

As the years passed, the coalition suffered mounting losses as well. More than 4,400 American troops and 180 British troops had died in Iraq by late 2010, along with thousands of Iraqi security forces personnel. Because the Iraqi security forces—which had grown to number 600,000 by 2010— seemed finally able to keep the peace, many

Shiites, such as this Baghdad family, were long oppressed by Saddam Hussein, and many were attacked by al Qaeda or Sunnis after his fall.

## SUNNI VS. SHIA

Muslims are divided into two main sects, or groups: Sunni and Shia. Worldwide, Sunnis (Muslims who revere Abu Bakr, a prominent disciple of the prophet Muhammad, as Muhammad's successor) make up about 80 percent of Muslims; Shiites (Muslims who believe that Muhammad designated his son-in-law, Ali ibn Abi Talib, as his successor) make up about 20 percent. In Iraq, however, the majority of people are Shiites, while the government under Saddam Hussein was ruled by Sunnis. As of 2011, fighting between Shiites and Sunnis continued to undermine the stability of Iraq's new democratic government.

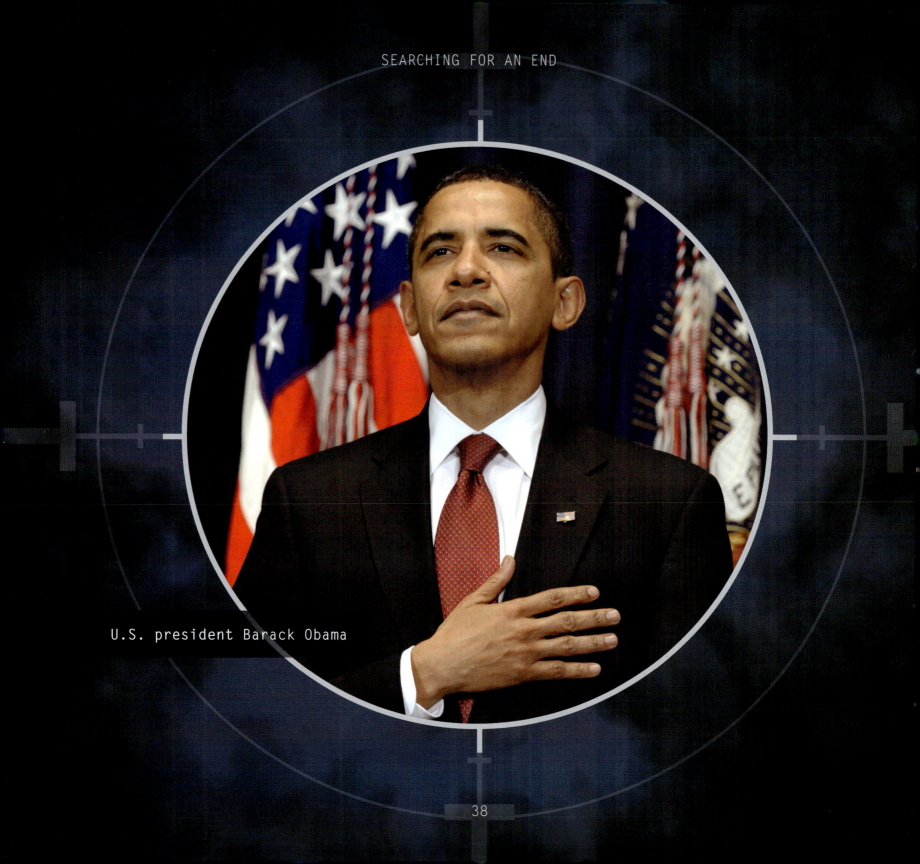

U.S. president Barack Obama

war-weary Americans, including some members of Congress, began calling for the U.S. to leave Iraq. New president Barack Obama, who took office in January 2009, announced that American combat troops would be withdrawn from Iraq by the fall of 2010, with other security and intelligence personnel leaving a year later. All other coalition nations withdrew their troops by early 2010.

Yet while an end to the Iraq War seemed within reach, the situation in Afghanistan began to worsen. Because key troops had been withdrawn from Afghanistan in 2002 to prepare for the invasion of Iraq, the Taliban had survived the U.S.-led coalition's initial onslaught and managed to regroup. By mid-2008, Taliban insurgents had grown to number about 25,000 and were increasingly

launching bombing attacks in urban areas of Afghanistan and along the Afghanistan-Pakistan border. The increase in Taliban attacks prompted some U.S. officials, including Obama and secretary of state Hillary Clinton, to suggest that Pakistan—despite vowing after 9/11 to cooperate with the coalition—only occasionally pursued the Taliban in earnest, more frequently taking a relaxed approach to the insurgents. As Pakistani journalist Ahmed Rashid noted, "It appeared that the Afghan Taliban were set on a finely tuned strategy, with the Pakistan army turning a blind eye to it."

Facing increased pressure from the coalition in 2008, Pakistan's military increased its efforts to hunt down Taliban militants, capturing dozens of low-ranking commanders. However, the U.S. remained skeptical of Pakistan's commitment, and on September 3, 2008, a group of U.S. Special Forces soldiers landed by helicopter near Angor Adda in South Waziristan, Pakistan, launching a raid that resulted in the deaths of 25 Taliban militants and as many as 20 civilians. The incident, which was the first overt U.S. ground attack on Pakistani soil, infuriated Pakistani officials and citizens. It also was condemned by European leaders such as French president Nicolas Sarkozy and German chancellor Angela Merkel (whose countries belonged to the **North Atlantic Treaty Organization (NATO)** and therefore contributed troops to the war in Afghanistan), who argued that the key to building trust among the Afghan people

was reconstruction efforts, not increased military action.

The Bush administration had alienated many countries around the world with policies that often seemed inclined toward combat rather than diplomacy. As Bush's presidency neared its end in 2008, Illinois senator Barack Obama campaigned for president on a vow to end the wars in Iraq and Afghanistan as quickly as possible and bring the troops home. As an Illinois state senator, Obama had spoken against the 2003 invasion of Iraq, and he believed that the U.S. must regain international support in order to defeat terrorism and achieve lasting peace. When Obama was elected president in November 2008, many people around the world celebrated. He echoed the thoughts of many

## STATUES DESTROYED

In March 2001, the Taliban further alienated the Afghan public and the leaders of foreign countries when it began destroying pre-Islamic, ancient statues throughout Afghanistan. Taliban leader Mullah Muhammad Omar stated that these statues—including two 2,000-year-old statues of the religious figure Buddha—represented false idols and that their presence violated Islamic law. Despite international outcry, the Taliban completed its demolition in a few short weeks, further strengthening its hold on Afghanistan.

These Taliban insurgents in Afghanistan were photographed shortly after they ambushed and killed 10 French soldiers in August 2008.

## POPPY POWER

Afghanistan is the 219th poorest nation among the world's 229, and an important source of income for many farmers and drug lords is opium. Corruption in the Afghan government and widespread poverty throughout the country caused opium production to skyrocket nearly 200 percent between 2002 and 2008. Some of the opium was used in Afghanistan—30 percent of the Taliban's income came from drug trafficking in 2008—but much of it was smuggled into the West and sold illegally, where it could be converted into other drugs such as heroin or morphine.

Because Afghanistan farming typically involves entire families, the rise of opium in the country drew many children into the drug trade.

when he stated in his January 2009 inaugural address that "our power alone cannot protect us, nor does it entitle us to do as we please."

However, withdrawing American troops from Afghanistan proved to be more difficult than Obama expected. By late 2009, it seemed to many people in the coalition nations and beyond that an end to the war in Afghanistan remained very distant. Afghan president Hamid Karzai's government was deeply flawed, plagued with charges that government

Afghan president Hamid Karzai

officials, court justices, and police officers accepted bribes from Afghan drug lords. This, along with a lack of coalition security support, made many Afghans lose confidence in their government's ability to curb the crime and bloodshed. Although many Afghans did not agree with the Taliban's violent tactics, some chose to fight with them because they believed they would receive no protection if they spoke out against them. Adding to the difficulty of the situation was the fact that, in 2009, the Afghan army and police force had fewer than 200,000 members, far short of the estimated 400,000 that U.S. General Stanley McChrystal said would be needed to secure the country.

Despite his goals of withdrawing U.S. forces from Afghanistan, Obama in December 2009 pledged an additional 30,000 troops to be deployed throughout early 2010, which brought the U.S. troop total in Afghanistan to just under 100,000. This decision was controversial to many Americans who had voted for Obama, as he appeared to renege on his campaign promise. Despite the general unpopularity of the war, America's NATO allies, who had a combined 38,000 troops stationed in Afghanistan in late 2009, were supportive of the U.S. plans, although many nations were reluctant to commit more of their own forces. Obama assured the public that U.S. troops would begin withdrawing from Afghanistan in July 2011, but many critics considered that timeline overly optimistic and likely to leave Afghanistan a still-unstable country.

The War on Terror, because it involves a global, stateless enemy, has been unlike any war fought before. As America and its Western allies sought new ways to both bring terrorists to justice and to protect their homelands, numerous debates arose about what is fair, what is reasonable, and what is ethical. And as terrorist groups such as al Qaeda used Islam to justify barbaric acts against the West and even against fellow Muslims, peaceable followers of Islam were forced to defend the tenets of their religion. As the war goes on, new controversies are sure to arise, further complicating an already complex struggle.

Many devoted and peaceable Muslims believe that the violent actions of fundamentalist groups have harmed the image of Islam.

## THE MUSLIM BROTHERHOOD

The Muslim Brotherhood—an Islamic fundamentalist group—was founded by schoolteacher Hassan al-Banna in Egypt in the 1920s with the goal of instituting Islamic law in the governments of all Muslim-majority countries. At first, the Brotherhood used religious groups to achieve political reform. However, in 1948, a member of the Brotherhood was accused of assassinating Egyptian prime minister Mahmud Fahmi Nokrashi. After the Egyptian government banned the Brotherhood in 1954, it split into different factions. Today, more than 70 branches exist worldwide—some, such as Palestine's Hamas, use terrorist bombings to spread their jihadist message.

**absolute monarchy** — a form of government in which a king or queen rules with absolute power and does not answer to any other governing body

**blasphemous** — describing irreverent behavior or statements made with no regard for religion

**burkas** — loose garments covering the entire body, with a veiled opening only for the eyes, traditionally worn by Muslim women when they are in public

**coalition** — an alliance of individuals or groups who join together for a common cause

**Cold War** — a prolonged rivalry between the Soviet Union and its communist supporters and the U.S. and its democratic allies; it lasted from about 1947 to 1991

**collateral damage** — accidental harm done to innocent civilians or their property during military combat

**court-martialed** — put on trial before a court consisting of appointed military personnel, usually in cases of offenses by soldiers or sailors

**Geneva Conventions** — a series of international agreements, first made in Geneva, Switzerland, in 1864, that established rules for the fair and humane treatment of prisoners of war and of troops injured in battle

**habeas corpus** — a formal document requiring a jailed person to be brought before a judge or court; it is used as protection against illegal imprisonment

**insurgents** — people who fight or otherwise actively participate in a revolt or uprising against a government or ruling force

**intelligence** — information concerning political or military matters, including potential acts by an enemy or possible enemy

**jihadists** — Muslims who participate in a holy war waged as a religious duty against people who do not believe in Islam

**militants** — people who use aggression or combat in support of a cause

**military tribunals** — military courts organized in time of war to try offenses by individuals who are not subject to trial by a court-martial

**mujahideen** — a military force of Muslim guerrilla fighters; the word is Arabic for "holy warriors" and refers in particular to fighters during Afghanistan's resistance to Soviet occupation from 1979 to 1989

**North Atlantic Treaty Organization (NATO)** — an alliance of 28 countries in North America and Europe that provides political or military support to protect its member countries

**Pentagon** — a huge, five-sided building near Washington, D.C., that is the headquarters of the U.S. Department of Defense

**regime** — a government in power or prevailing system of government; the term often has a negative and oppressive implication

**secretary of state** — the U.S. president's chief foreign affairs adviser, who often meets with leaders and ambassadors of other countries for diplomatic talks and negotiations

**unilateralism** — the tendency of nations to conduct their foreign affairs individually, without the involvement or consent of other nations

**United Nations (UN)** — an organization with representatives from 192 nations that deals with international law, human rights, and economic progress, and aims to maintain peace between nations through communication

**UN Security Council** — a body of the UN composed of representatives from 15 countries; the Security Council can pass resolutions that authorize war or impose economic penalties upon countries

**weapons of mass destruction (WMD)** — weapons such as nuclear bombs and chemicals or gases that are capable of killing large numbers of people or destroying huge areas

ENDNOTES

Cole, David. *Justice at War: The Men and Ideas That Shaped America's War on Terror*. New York: New York Review Books, 2008.

Honigsberg, Peter Jan. *Our Nation Unhinged: The Human Consequences of the War on Terror*. Berkeley, Calif.: University of California Press, 2009.

Kepel, Gilles, and Jean-Pierre Milelli, eds. Translated by Pascale Ghazaleh. *Al Qaeda in Its Own Words*. Cambridge, Mass.: Belknap Press of Harvard University Press, 2008.

Khosrokhavar, Farhad. *Inside Jihadism: Understanding Jihadi Movements Worldwide*. Boulder, Colo.: Paradigm Publishers, 2009.

# SELECTED BIBLIOGRAPHY

McKelvey, Tara. *Monstering: Inside America's Policy of Secret Interrogations and Torture in the Terror War*. New York: Carroll & Graf, 2007.

National Commission on Terrorist Attacks Upon the United States. *The 9/11 Commission Report: Final Report of the National Commission on Terrorist Attacks upon the United States.* New York: W. W. Norton, 2004.

Riedel, Bruce. *The Search for al Qaeda: Its Leadership, Ideology, and Future*. Washington, D.C.: Brookings Institution Press, 2008.

Roy, Olivier. *The Politics of Chaos in the Middle East*. New York: Columbia University Press, 2008.